WHAT I FEEL

I AM HAPPY

Beth Gottlieb

first concepts

Gareth Stevens
PUBLISHING

I am happy!

Mom gives me a hug.

I am happy!

Nana calls me.
I am happy!

I run at the park.

I am happy!

I see Sam.

I am happy!

Dad and I walk the dog.
I am happy!

I get wet.

I am happy!

I eat ice cream.

I am happy!

I get a new book.

I am happy!

I fly a kite.

I am happy!

What makes
you feel happy?

Please visit our website, www.garethstevens.com. For a free color catalog of all our high-quality books, call toll free 1-800-542-2595 or fax 1-877-542-2596.

Library of Congress Cataloging-in-Publication Data

Names: Gottlieb, Beth author
Title: I am happy / Beth Gottlieb.
Description: Buffalo, New York : Gareth Stevens Publishing, [2027] | Series: What I feel
Identifiers: LCCN 2025027199 (print) | LCCN 2025027200 (ebook) | ISBN 9781482476064 (library binding) | ISBN 9781482476057 (paperback) | ISBN 9781482476071 (ebook)
Subjects: LCSH: Happiness in children–Juvenile literature | Happiness–Juvenile literature | Emotions in children–Juvenile literature | LCGFT: Literature
Classification: LCC BF723.H37 G68 2027 (print) | LCC BF723.H37 (ebook) | DDC 155.4/1242–dc23/eng/20250804
LC record available at https://lccn.loc.gov/2025027199
LC ebook record available at https://lccn.loc.gov/2025027200

Published in 2027 by
Gareth Stevens Publishing
2544 Clinton Street
Buffalo, NY 14224

Designer: Deanna Lepovich
Editor: Therese Shea

Photo credits: Cover Tartila/Shutterstock.com; cover, pp. 3, 5, 7, 9, 11, 13, 15, 17, 19, 21, 23 (texture) v_kulieva/Shutterstock.com; p. 3 Rido/Shutterstock.com; p. 5 Dmytro Hai/Shutterstock.com; p. 7 NaMong Productions92/Shutterstock.com; p. 9 Pixel-Shot/Shutterstock.com; p. 11 Dmytro Zinkevych/Shutterstock.com; p. 13 Irina WS/Shutterstock.com; p. 15 FamVeld/Shutterstock.com; p. 17 ShineTerra/Shutterstock.com; p. 19 Evgeny Atamanenko/Shutterstock.com; p. 21 Sorapop Udomsri/Shutterstock.com; p. 23 Rawpixel.com/Shutterstock.com.

Printed in China

CPSIA compliance information: Batch #QSGS27: For further information contact Gareth Stevens at 1-800-542-2595.